FIRSTS
AND
FOREMOSTS

First edition for the United States, Canada,
and the Philippines published 1992
by Barron's Educational Series, Inc.

© Copyright by Aladdin Books Ltd 1992

Design David West Children's Book Design
Illustrator David West
Text Anita Ganeri
Picture research Emma Krikler

Created and designed by
N.W. Books
28 Percy Street
London W1P 9FF

All inquiries should be addressed to:
Barron's Educational Series, Inc.
250 Wireless Boulevard
Hauppauge, NY 11788

International Standard Book No. 0-8120-6292-2

Library of Congress Catalog No. 92-13282

Library of Congress Cataloging-in-Publication Data

Ganeri, Anita, 1961-
Firsts and foremosts / Anita Ganeri : illustrator, David West, -- 1st ed.
p. cm. -- (Questions and answers about--)
Summary: Cartoons and color photographs accompany answers to
questions about some of the first or foremost record breakers.
ISBN 0-8120-6292-2
1. Curiosities and wonders--Juvenile literature. 2. World
records--Juvenile literature. 3. Children's questions and answers.
[1. World records--Miscellanea. 2. Questions and answers.]
I. West, David, ill. II. Title. III. Series: Ganeri, Anita, 1961-
Questions and answers about--
AG243.G284 1992
031.02--dc20   92-13282   CIP   AC

Printed in Belgium
234 987654321

QUESTIONS AND ANSWERS ABOUT
FIRSTS
AND
FOREMOSTS

Barron's

Firsts and Foremosts

Thomas Edison invented the first electric light bulb in 1879. He was a very busy man. He invented over a thousand new objects in his lifetime. They included a record player and an electric pen. This book will help you to learn about some of the very first things of their kind. They include planes, trains, computers, telephones and space journeys.

Who was the first person to fly in a powered plane?

On December 17, 1903, Orville Wright became the first person to fly in an engine-driven aircraft. He flew his plane, Flyer 1, for 120 feet (36.5 meters) at a speed of almost 30 miles (48 kilometers) an hour. The flight lasted for just 12 seconds. Orville was watched by his brother, Wilbur, who had built the plane with him.

Who were the first passengers in a hot-air balloon?

The French Montgolfier brothers launched the first passenger-carrying hot-air balloon in 1783. But the passengers were not people. They were a sheep, a duck, and a rooster. They returned to earth safely after their amazing flight.

Who was the first person to discover America?

Christopher Columbus is thought to have been the first European to discover America. He left Spain with three small sailing ships in August 1492. He sighted land two months later. But Columbus was sure he had landed in Asia. No one could ever change his mind.

Who was the first person to sail around the world?

In 1519, Ferdinand Magellan set off from Seville, Spain, with five ships and 250 men. In 1522, only one ship and 18 men returned home – without Magellan, who was killed during the voyage. They had sailed right around the world, a distance of almost 40,000 miles (64,000 kilometers).

When was the first bicycle built?

The first pedal bicycle was built in 1839 by Kirkpatrick Macmillan, a Scottish blacksmith. It was called a velocipede, which means "swift foot." It had pedals attached to rods that made the back wheel turn.

What was the first motor car offered for sale?

The Motorwagen was the first car offered for sale to run on gasoline. It was built by the German inventor and engineer, Karl-Friedrich Benz, in 1885. The car had three wheels. It had a top speed of 10 miles (16 kilometers) an hour.

Where did the first steam locomotive run?

The first steam locomotive was built in 1803 by an English engineer, called Richard Trevithick. It was supposed to run on a railway track in Shropshire, England but there are no records of this. Trevithick built another locomotive in 1804.
It ran for the first time in Wales.

Who made the first steam engine?

The first steam engine ever was designed by Hero of Alexandria about 2,000 years ago. It was made of a hollow, metal ball filled with water. This was heated over a fire. The force of the steam coming out of its sides made the ball turn around.

Which was the first plane to fly faster than the speed of sound?

In 1947, the USA's Bell XS-1 rocket plane flown by Captain Charles Yeager became the first supersonic plane. Supersonic means that it flies faster than the speed of sound. The plane was nicknamed "Glamorous Glennis" after the pilot's wife!

Which was the first plane to fly passengers faster than the speed of sound? Concorde is the first and only supersonic passenger plane in the world. Concorde usually flies at 1,450 miles (2,333 kilometers) an hour – over twice the speed of sound. It can fly from New York to London in about three hours. An ordinary jet plane takes about twice as long.

U.S. AIR FORCE
6062

What did the first writing look like?

The very first people to write things down were the Sumerians. They lived in the Middle East about 5,500 years ago. They used pictures to show words. About 5,000 years ago, the ancient Egyptians invented a type of writing called hieroglyphics. Picture-like symbols were used for whole words, parts of words, or sounds.

What did people first use as money?

Long before coins were invented, people used stones, metal bars, shells, and animals as money. They exchanged them for other goods. The first coins were made in Turkey over 2,200 years ago. They were lumps of metal with the royal seal stamped on them.

Who designed the first computer?

An English mathematician, Charles Babbage, designed the first computing machine in 1834. But it was too complicated to build! The machine was designed to store the results of long, difficult calculations. Its operator would have turned a handle to make it work. Babbage's machine led the way for the invention of modern calculators and computers.

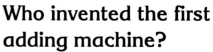

Who invented the first adding machine?

Abacuses were the first machines for adding. They were invented about 5,000 years ago by the Chinese or Babylonians. An abacus is made of a wooden frame with rows of beads on rods. The beads count as ones, tens, hundreds, and thousands.

Who was the first man to walk on the Moon?

On July 21, 1969, the American astronaut, Neil Armstrong, became the first person to walk on the Moon. He stepped out of the Apollo 11 lunar module onto the Sea of Tranquility at 2:56 am. He was followed onto the Moon by another astronaut, Edwin Aldrin.

Who were the first humans to walk upright?

In 1978, scientists discovered a track of footprints in Tanzania, Africa. They were made about 3.5 million years ago by three ape men. They are the earliest signs we have of our ancestors walking upright.

Who made the first phone call?

The first telephone was invented and used by Alexander Graham Bell in 1876. He discovered a way of sending speech signals through a wire. The first long-distance phone calls were made in 1884, between New York and Boston. Today there are about 425 million telephones in the world.

When were the first television pictures shown?

A Scottish engineer, called John Logie Baird, produced the first television pictures in 1926 – in his attic! The pictures were of a boy who had been passing by in the street. John Logie Baird had dashed out and asked for his help.

Who was the first person in space?

A Russian cosmonaut, Yuri Gagarin, was the first person to go into space. In 1961, he circled once around Earth in his spaceship, Vostok 1. He flew at a height of 203 miles (327 kilometers) above the ground. The flight only lasted for 108 minutes, but it proved that people could survive traveling in space.

When was the first satellite launched?

The first satellite was launched in 1957. It was called Sputnik 1. There are hundreds of satellites in orbit around Earth today. They are used to send television pictures and telephone calls around the world. They are also used for collecting information about the weather.

Who were the first artists?

The world's first artists were prehistoric people who lived about 40,000 years ago. They decorated cave walls with pictures of the animals they hunted. These included bulls, mammoths, buffalos, and horses. In the Lascaux Caves in France, the walls are covered with nearly 600 animal paintings.

What was the first camera like? The first camera was called a camera obscura. It was discovered about 1,000 years ago. It was a large dark box or darkened room with a small hole in its side or wall. Light from an object went through the hole and projected an image of the object on to a screen inside.

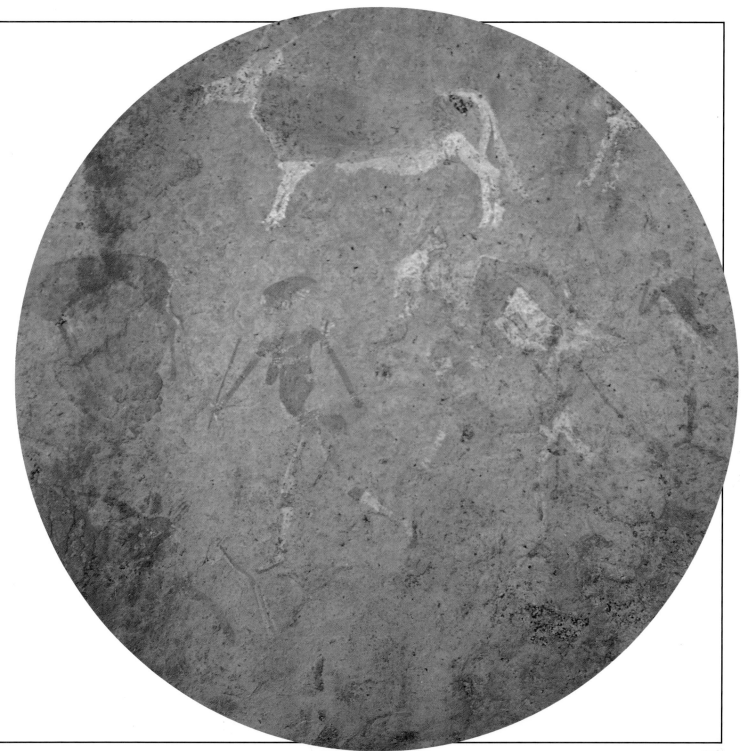

Index